M000101799

Yellow Umbrella Books are published by Capstone Press
151 Good Counsel Drive, P.O. Box 669, Mankato, Minnesota 56002
http://www.capstone-press.com

Library of Congress Cataloging-in-Publication Data
Tucker, Shirley.
    Odd and even numbers/by Shirley Tucker and Jane Rambo.
    p. cm. — (Math)
    Includes index.
    Summary: Simple text and photographs introduce the properties of odd and even
numbers.
    ISBN 0-7368-1286-5
    1. Numbers, Natural—Juvenile literature. 2. Arithmetic. [1. Numbers, Natural.] I. Rambo,
Jane. II. Title. III. Series.
QA141.3 .T83 2002
513.2—dc21   2002016827

Editorial Credits
Susan Evento, Managing Editor/Product Development; Elizabeth Jaffe, Senior Editor; Charles
Hunt, Designer; Kimberly Danger and Heidi Schoof, Photo Researchers
Photo Credits
Cover: Scott Campbell/International Stock; Title Page: Uniphoto; Page 2: David F. Clobes; Page 3:
David F. Clobes (left and right); Page 4: Wally Eberhart/Visuals Unlimited (top left), Bruce
Berg/Visuals Unlimited (top right), John Sohlden/Visuals Unlimited (bottom right), Unicorn
Stock (bottom left); Page 5: Uniphoto (top left), William Palmer/Visuals Unlimited (top middle),
Jeff Greenberg/Visuals Unlimited (top right), Cheryl A. Ertelt (bottom right), Mark S.
Skalny/Visuals Unlimited (bottom left); Page 6: Larry Dunmire/Photo Network (top), M&D
Long/Visuals Unlimited (bottom); Page 7: Anthony Mercieca/Root Resources (top left), Frank
Armstrong/Photo Network (top right), Aneal Vohra/Unicorn Stock (bottom right), Dee
Culleny/Visuals Unlimited (top left); Page 8: Frank Armstrong/Photo Network (top), Cheryl
Ertelt (bottom), Page 9: Inga Spence/Visuals Unlimited (top left), Roger Cole/Visuals Unlimited
(top right), R. Al Simpson/Visuals Unlimited (bottom right), Phyllis Kedl/Unicorn Stock (bottom
left); Page 11: Tom McCarthy/Unicorn Stock; Page 12: Sunstar/International Stock; Page 13: Jeff
Greenberg/Visuals Unlimited (top), Kent & Donna Dannen (bottom); Page 14: Jeff Daly/Visuals
Unlimited (top), Jakub Jasinski/Visuals Unlimited; Page 15: Cheryl Ertelt (top and bottom), Page
16: Fritz Polking/Bruce Coleman

Odd and Even Numbers

By Jane Rambo and Dr.Shirley Tucker

Consulting Editor: Gail Saunders-Smith, Ph.D.
Consultants: Claudine Jellison and Patricia Williams,
Reading Recovery Teachers
Content Consultant: Johanna Kaufman,
Math Learning/Resource Director of the Dalton School

These are whole numbers.

1 3 5 7 9
0 2 4 6 8

We use these whole numbers
to write any whole numbers.

10   35   68   47
100   8   24   9

Whole numbers can belong to two different sets.

Odd Set:
1 3 5 7 9

Even Set:
0 2 4 6 8

3

The Even Set

0   2   4   6   8

Except for **0**, even numbers can be grouped into sets of **2**s, called pairs.

2 tulips

4 kittens

6 kids

8 eggs

The Odd Set

1 3 5 7 9

Except for **1**, odd numbers can be grouped in pairs with **1** left over.

1 duck

5 eggs

9 helmets

7 crayons

3 puppies

Here are **2** feet.

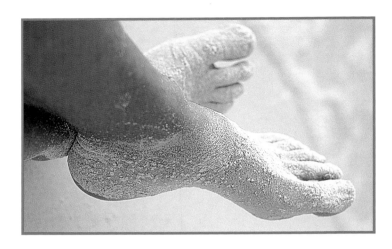

Here are **12** eggs.

These are even numbers.

Which numbers below are even numbers?

3 eggs

4 kids

2 kittens

1 puppy

A tricycle has **3** wheels.

Here are **5** sisters.

These are odd numbers.

Which numbers below are odd numbers?

3 apples

4 tulips

3 swings

5 geese

Here are whole numbers
on a number line.

0 1 2 3 4 5 6 7 8 9

Odd numbers are always
found between even numbers
on a number line.
To tell if numbers are even or
odd, look at the ones' place.

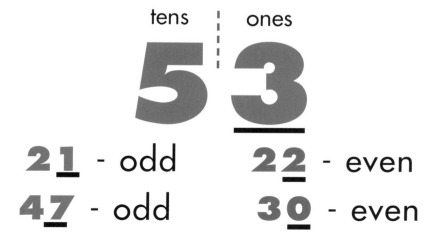

tens ¦ ones

5 3

2**1** - odd   2**2** - even

4**7** - odd   3**0** - even

There are **13** students
in this class going to lunch.
Is **13** an even or odd number?
Look at the ones' place to
help you decide.

This class is in the park.
There are **12** students.

Is **12** an odd or even number?
Look at the ones' place
to help you decide.

Now let's see what happens
to odd and even numbers
when we add them.
If we add two even numbers,
we get an even number.

4 kids

+ **2** kids
_____
= **6** kids

If we add two odd numbers,
we get an even number.
Let's try it!

3 cherries

+ 1 cherry

= 4 cherries

If I add one even number
and one odd number,
is the sum even or odd?
Let's try it.

4 dogs

+ **3** dogs

= **7** dogs

Every whole number is either odd or even.
If it's even, it is **0** or can be grouped into perfect sets of **2**s, called pairs.
If it's odd, it is **1** or can be grouped in pairs with **1** left over.

Words to Know/Index

Word Count: 286
Early-Intervention Level:12